TEN (MODERN) ZEN TIPS

for online leadership

DR. LIZ MUSIL

INTRODUCTION

When you are leading a team online, you don't have the luxury of physical contact to create engagement, build cohesiveness, and develop relationships. Modes of communication such as facial expressions, tonality of speech, body language, and feedback are replaced by interactive technology. With a growing number of organizations operating in the cloud, the need for successful leadership in virtual settings is increasing. New skills need to be embraced to ensure successful behaviors, skills, and attributes of leadership are practiced.

Although online entrepreneurship has grown significantly over the past decade, limited information is available on how to successfully lead a virtual business. Online leadership continues to challenge entrepreneurs with shifting requirements and technological innovation. Businesses operating in the cloud face a serious deficiency as entrepreneurs often lack the crucial skills needed to lead and manage in the virtual environment.

UNDERSTANDING THE VIRTUAL ENVIRONMENT

Leadership in the online environment requires that the entrepreneur overcomes communication challenges that can occur when managing online. Without face to face interaction, it can be tricky to create engagement, challenge a team, spark interest in the project and meet goals. New models need to be created to define the behaviors, skills, and attributes of a successful leader in an online setting.

Differentiating average and exceptional virtual leaders in business is similar to the recognizing the difference between mediocre and professional musicians. A mediocre piano player may be technically precise, but lack the intuitiveness and ease of a professional musician. Likewise, an online entrepreneur may exhibit the behavior and skill of a virtual leader. However, data from studies suggested that highly effective virtual leaders intuitively display 'constellations' of attributes. By effectively blending core attributes, these leaders build a collaborative online culture that furthers business objectives.

What is a Virtual Leader?

Scholars and researchers can address virtual leadership is a multi-disciplinary construct. Data from studies indicate that virtual leadership requires mastery of technological as well as people skills. Unlike face-to-face teamwork, virtual collaboration intertwines technology and communication. From a business perspective, virtual commerce continues to flourish. While brick-and-mortar businesses continue to operate profitably, a growing number of organizations deliver services in a virtual environment (e.g., online course, webinars, coaching, e-books). Understandably, synchronous and asynchronous communication is critical in a virtual environment.

Virtual leadership is the practice of leading an organization in a virtual environment regardless whether the organization is hybrid or virtual. Cloud based teams are increasingly being created in organizations that can span time and distance, taking on new challenges of globalization. Effective virtual leadership encompasses the leadership of virtual teams by increasing the trust of stakeholders working remotely, and reducing process losses by effectively using technology. A virtual team leader leads a virtual team asynchronously and synchronously using electronic means of communication.

What is successful leadership in the online environment?

Contemporary examples of successful leadership in the online environment can be observed in several organizations. Leaders of successful virtual organizations consistently demonstrate communication and interpersonal skills to complement technology. LinkedIn CEO Jeff Weiner is an example of an inspirational and motivational leader with outstanding results. The company currently has a 92% approval rating with over 3,000 employees and 200 million members. A key to Weiner's success is melding technology with empathetic treatment of employees (Morrison, 2013).

Another example of exemplary virtual leadership is Zappos CEO Tony Hsieh. He developed Zappos Family Core Values that outline the organization's brand, culture, and business strategies. Zappos grew rapidly with a Hsieh's hands-off approach to leadership, who leads by creating a "positive team and family spirit" (Duncan, 2013, para. 4). Similarly, Evernote's CEO Phil Libin's leadership approach endeavors to promote communication and remove obstacles. Libin is described as having a warm, embracing personality (Wang, 2013).

1.
LEAD
DIFFERENTLY

The five major elements to be implemented for successful, synergistic cloud based teams are: lead differently, impose trust building, communication, develop your skill set, and use global decision making. Synergistic cloud-based teams are visible in all virtual organizations by the borderless interaction facilitated by technology, creating compounded cultures that are volatile, and challenging to lead.

These concepts translate to the online blog or business, which interacts as a synergistic team to sell products and services. Online leadership calls for entrepreneurs to create momentum by working ahead of the group by introducing concepts, tasks, and challenges. Online facilitation calls for nurturing and development by fostering independence and interdependence, while balancing both. It is vital for virtual leaders to communicate both synchronously asynchronously, and understand the frequency of communication needed in various business situations. They should model behaviors such as patience, flexibility, maturity, and self- management. Too often, online business is reactionary to blog comments and sales. Virtual business leadership encourages relationships, engagement, and interaction by providing many opportunities for participation.

I behave similarly online as I do when I work face to face. I try to be a trailblazer, set high standards, and convey that I expect them to be met. I aspire for the best and encourage the same for my clients. I practice confidence and high self-esteem. This translates to strong planning and organization of business projects, attention to detail, and communicating effectively online. Strong writing and technical skills are demonstrated as well as follow up and meetings. I build relationships one on one, and with the group.

To be effective, especially when managing people and projects online, it is important to figure out just how much to communicate to inform people of what they need to know. You need to not over-manage and not under-manage. Never leave your clients guessing about goals, processes, objectives, and roles. Sharing deadlines and information can give people necessary information to feel part of the group, if appropriate. Be inclusive, professional, objective, and kind.

— 2. —

think
CREATIVELY

Getting on board with technology is critical to take advantage the online environment. As a blogger and entrepreneur working online, it's beneficial to consistently try new software and programs that may enhance the classroom. Take advantage of videos and interactive tools that convey learning objectives in a variety of ways. Clients are stimulated with a variety of experiences, so an absolute must is great communication via written word, presentations, online chats, videos and Skype. Be able to communicate clearly, to the point, supplemented by notes. Convey goals and responsibilities clearly. Make sure there is communication that is positive and the others feels their contributions are valued. Promote a dynamic business vibe with a greater reliance on tools available online.

3.

understand
YOUR ROLES
and
responsibilities

When leading any business, the most important thing is a clarity of purpose - a very clear sense of what the objectives of your business are. Communication of the overall products and services as a positive, upbeat manner serves to build a good online work relationship. When working and presenting oneself online this becomes even more important, because there is no (or little) face to face contact, so the purpose and energy of the work has to be entirely conveyed online. Everything communicated needs to be checked against this core purpose/energy.

Most importantly is upholding professionalism online, while also being relaxed and human. It's often beneficial to use social media to connect with groups, but keep it respectful. Get to know your clients, peers, and competitors, communicate with them in a respectful, firm, but kind tone. Build relationships one on one and with the group. Adjust the level and frequency of communication based on the situation. Have one on one phone meetings and emails to bond and answer questions. Document the assignment roles, goals, timeline. Promote, high level quality business experiences helps build a successful client base.

4.

create engagement

AND BUILD

community

The core is communication to creating engagement, building community, and online tech tools. Technical skills and communication skills dominate virtual work. Good communication skills are essential, and an ability to anticipate what reactions might be to a particular topic or statement, and/or how it may be misunderstood. Especially when it comes to written online communications, there is such a big possibility of miscommunication due to the lack of body language and facial cues. It is essential to make communications very clear, and to be able to place yourself in your potential audience/reader's minds.

Responsiveness is also key, responding to comments or questions in a timely manner, and to emails and forum posts when managing your blog, so that participants feel that the connection is as 'real-time' as possible. Frequent communication both synchronous and asynchronous to motivate, get to know your followers, and gain control. Encourage self- management and self-esteem in all interactions, while setting the tone of your business transactions through the type, frequency, and content of your communications. Effective entrepreneurs are particularly good at bringing together people to communicate with each other and to feel part of a group.

5.

master

A VARIETY

OF TECHNICAL TOOLS

Communication in the cloud is supported with technical tools such as email, tools within learning management systems, Skype, video, and synchronous webinars. Entrepreneurs online can supplement asynchronous tools with individual or team synchronous communications. Using technical tools effectively require connections between soft skills and hard skills. For example, the frequency and method of communication using virtual tools such as Skype, email, chats, and online meetings create communication opportunities using various levels of media richness. An example would be clarifying a skill via email followed up with a group synchronous online meeting. Soft skills, such as emotional intelligence, intent, fairness, and reliability, are vital regardless of the medium used to communicate.

6. COMMUNICATE
CLEARLY, RESPONSIVELY,
and effectively

Good online communication requires planning ahead and organization. Clients, co-workers, and peers need clear, timely instructions, support, and feedback. Flexibility is important, the communication style you use should fit the circumstances. Virtual commerce is often global and spans across various time zones, so mindfulness of scheduling synchronous communication is important.

Balance opportunities for growth with assignment tasks. Use communication tools to motivate your team and to monitor progress virtually. Practice strong technical and people skills as an influencer and group cheerleader. Demand a high level of respect among all stakeholders. Communicate clearly, keep tone friendly and professional. Use technology wisely to move projects forward. Praise good work, show that you are dependable and articulate. Establish trust and motivation. Don't micromanage but follow up frequently. Keep clear boundaries with social media and enforce policies that govern online behavior and netiquette.

7.

BE EMOTIONALLY INTELLIGENT

Emotional intelligence, management, and leadership merge as a single business concept because of the global, technically driven, politically charged, flexible environment today's organizations must compete in. Leadership principles continue to be refined as they are affect positive change towards the effectiveness of a coaching session, course, or sales effort. Virtual entrepreneurs work in a boundary-less milieu supported by strategic alliances and the Internet. The entire tone of an online business is driven by the emotional intelligence of the entrepreneur who must demonstrate emotional self-management, empathy, communication, and experience.

★

8.
be
self-directed
and lead
others to
be self-directed

★

Critical to online business independence, self-direction, and mixing autonomy with strategic use of resources. Entrepreneurs need to promote independent thought, research, and problem solving among clients, peers, and competitors. Virtual entrepreneurs should not create dependencies. Instead, they train the people they interact with to be independent and self-reliant. Again, the interrelationship between hard and soft skills emerges, positive communication using technology effectively supported by emotional intelligence.

9.

organization and planning are
critical

Organization and planning serves the online business in several ways. Online entrepreneurs must take time to learn the various communication styles of their clients. Business owners should practice efficient time management, and proficient in using technology tools. Having good writing skills and explaining procedures and processes correctly the first time will prevent back and forth emails seeking clarification. Proficiency in computer applications increases productivity as project management tools can be used to facilitate grading and team management. Positive, diplomatic communications using simple netiquette can diffuse misunderstanding in the discussion threads. Organization in communication is also critical to bond with clients, build relationships and establish trust. Entrepreneurs should monitor teams towards appropriate use of power, meeting deadlines, achieving goals, and success. Projects can be articulated towards the proper breakdown of tasks, realistic time frames, and effective check in procedures with peers, employees, and alliances.

The technical aspect of organization encompasses managing the cloud, which is remote file management, security, version control, and other technical issues that may arise. Build flexibility in approaches to accommodate clients working with various tools such as laptops, tablets, and mobile devices. Offer assistance and tutorials to customers who need to develop their technical skills or are new to online business environments.

When you are leading online, it is important to influence via the frequency, type, and tone of interaction. A people orientation with strong technical skills moves the project forward. Show initiative, and lead by example by being accessible and not putting people off. Promptly reward successes, encourage all individuals equally, be visible online. Construct a regular schedule of communication individually, in groups, online, and by phone. Build a team culture with your business based on professionalism and personal development by organizing your communication interactions ahead of time. Manage problems and difficult situations promptly. Create the vision, mission, and values for your business and build that culture.

10.

BE OUTCOME
driven

Virtual leadership in an online business requires taking the technology, communication, emotional intelligence, and facilitation while being outcome driven. Support complex tasks, such as programming skills with supplemental tutorials and videos. Check in with quiet clients to make sure they are not falling behind. It's critical to make the online business environment safe and open enough that asking questions do not intimidate a client or employee. Don't stroke your own ego by making tasks unnecessarily complex or unnecessarily confusing. Be positive and clear. Validate information and support individuals without micromanaging or being absent. Show assertiveness when needed, and a sense of humor when needed. Be a people person but focus on tasks, keep the group on the work, and divide large goals into small chunks of work so people don't get overwhelmed. Create an online trail that is easy to follow with sequential links of information.

PUTTING IT ALL TOGETHER

Online entrepreneurs are trailblazers that practice their profession in the cloud, which is a communication medium that provides lower media richness than traditional business settings. From a business perspective, virtual commerce continues to flourish. While brick-and-mortar institutions continue to succeed, a growing number of organizations deliver products and services in a virtual environment (e.g., online course, webinars, coaching, products). Understandably, synchronous and asynchronous communication is critical in a virtual environment, and limitations created by the cloud must be overcome.

Successful virtual leadership in business requires that entrepreneurs are able to practice hard and soft skills to achieve goals. Leaders need to have strong communication, organizational, and technical skills to run a blog or online business. Unlike face-to-face businesses, virtual collaboration intertwines technology and communication. Flexibility in adapting new practices and technologies is also critical as online business is an emerging practice with varying demands. Various research studies on virtual leadership discuss constellations of behaviors, skills, and attributes are needed for success in the online environment.

The goals of leadership in virtual business are the same as the goals of traditional organizations. The environment in which business is conducted changed to the virtual world, requiring mastery of nontraditional functions in a global environment (Sheridan, 2012). Theorists and research supports the idea that virtual organizations continue to grow worldwide, calling for dispersed leadership, virtual teams, and virtual project management. Virtual leadership requires distinct abilities such as solid technology skills and effective communication over electronic tools with varying levels of media richness (Lojeski, 2010).

REFERENCES

Duncan, K. (2013, Feb).The positive influence. Retrieved from: http://www.entrepreneur.com/article/225804#hsieh

Lojeski, K. (2010). Leading the virtual workforce: How great leaders transform organizations in the 21st century. Retrieved from http://www.wiley.com/WileyCDA/Section/id-350044.html

Morrison, J. (2013, Feb).The constructive critic. Retrieved from: http://www.entrepreneur.com/article/225804#weiner

Musil, E. (2014) Leadership attributes for the virtual environment: A qualitative study (Doctoral dissertation). Retrieved from ProQuest Dissertations and Theses.

Sheridan, K. (2012). The virtual manager. Pompton Plains, NJ: The Career Press Inc.

Wang, J. (2013, Feb).The empowering force. Retrieved from: http://www.entrepreneur.com/article/225804#libi

About the author:

Dr. Liz Musil

Dr.Liz Musil is a virtual business coach, professor, consultant, author, public speaker and founder of Liz Musil Consultants. With over twenty years organizational, leadership, management, and technology consulting, and fifteen years' eCommerce and web development experience, Dr. Musil has an in depth understanding of leadership, management, and growth strategies for virtual organizations. She has worked in eCommerce, project management, strategy, finance, IT, and in all significant organizational capacities at the corporate level and as an external consultant.

Liz has consulted in entrepreneurial, virtual, and corporate business for over a decade in various industries such as education, banking, entertainment, music, and fashion. She also serves as an adjunct professor at several universities and has taught both in the classroom and online for over 12 years. Dr. Musil often is consulted as an instructional designer and a subject matter expert to develop online and classroom courses. Current projects include further researching Virtual Leadership attributes and creating research based assessment tools.

Dr. Liz Musil completed her Doctor of Management in Organizational Leadership from the University of Phoenix, and holds an M.A. in Organizational Management, a Masters in Information Technology, and a B.A. in Liberal Studies.

Liz spends most of her time in Southern California.

Please visit:

lizmusilconsultants.com
drlizmusil.com

www.ingramcontent.com/pod-product-compliance
Lightning Source LLC
Chambersburg PA
CBHW052049190326
41521CB00002BA/158